gift
wrapping

gift
wrapping

LUCY BERRIDGE *with text by* Charlotte Packer

photography by Carolyn Barber

RYLAND
PETERS
& SMALL

LONDON NEW YORK

For Jacob-Jude, who makes the sun shine every day...

Library of Congress Cataloging-in-Publication Data

Berridge, Lucy.
  Gift wrapping / Lucy Berridge with text by Charlotte Packer ; photography by Carolyn Barber.
    p. cm.
  ISBN 1-84172-689-3
  1. Gift wrapping. I. Title.
  TT870.B467 2004
  745.54–dc22

2004008825

Senior designer *Sally Powell*
Commissioning editor *Annabel Morgan*
Location researcher *Claire Hector*
Production *Paul Harding*
Art director *Gabriella Le Grazie*
Publishing director *Alison Starling*

Text *Charlotte Packer*

First published in the United States in 2004 by Ryland Peters & Small, Inc.
519 Broadway
5th Floor
New York, NY 10012
www.rylandpeters.com

Text, design, and photographs
© Ryland Peters & Small, Inc. 2004
10 9 8 7 6 5 4 3 2 1

Printed and bound in China.

contents

introduction

We give presents on many occasions and for many reasons, but whatever the gift is, whether it cost dollars or cents, it's important to give some thought to its presentation. Think of gift wrapping as a piece of theater—by wrapping presents artfully and imaginatively, you add to the pleasure friends and family will experience when receiving them.

There is an art to good gift wrapping, but it's an art that's easy to master—beautiful presentation is about taking the time to match your wrapping to the present and to the recipient. This book aims to inspire you to take a more creative approach and to show that good wrapping doesn't have to be complicated, just well-executed and appropriate to the gift and the occasion.

inspirations & materials

Think about the way that your favorite stores package their products and decide what you like and why, then consider how you can create the same pleasing effect. Once you consider the alternatives to a crumpled sheet of wrapping paper (secured with Scotch tape cut with your teeth because you've lost the scissors), you'll realize that the options are endless. When seeking inspiration, your search should start at home. What materials do you have at hand? This is the time to start collecting scraps of pretty paper, fabric and ribbon, sturdy boxes and gift bags.

below: **Subtle, neutral tones are enlivened with bold graphics or smart ribbon. Create a similar effect by ordering name tape bearing a message rather than your name.**

right: **Deceptively simple, this gift bag in a luscious shade of deep lilac is finished off with sheeny ribbon in the same hue. Rustling tissue paper adds to the sense of luxury.**

opposite: **The old-fashioned print on this box of chocolates is the key to its quirky charm, while the simplicity of a classic glass bottle with a chunky stopper is hard to beat.**

inspirations

Good packaging is designed to attract our attention and increase our desire for its contents—and this is exactly the effect you should aim for when wrapping a present.

The best wrapping and packaging that comes as part of a store-bought gift is timeless and understated, and its success lies in using materials of the very highest quality—thick grosgrain or satin ribbon, layers of subtly colored tissue paper and sturdy paper bags and boxes. Often items are cocooned luxuriously within their wrapping—buried beneath rustling sheets of tissue paper, or popped in a dinky little box and then inside a matching bag—and this luxe layering effect is easy to imitate.

Having looked at this sort of wrapping for inspiration, take it one stage further: hang on to gorgeous packaging and reuse it. Finding an elegant box when you need one is difficult, but removing or concealing tell-tale designer labels is easy.

Often items are cocooned luxuriously within their wrapping, and this layering effect is easy to imitate.

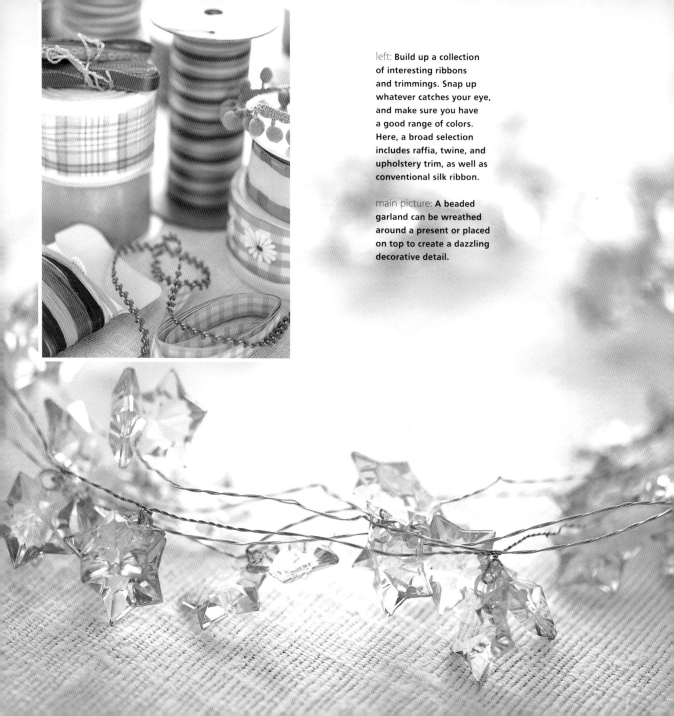

left: **Build up a collection of interesting ribbons and trimmings. Snap up whatever catches your eye, and make sure you have a good range of colors. Here, a broad selection includes raffia, twine, and upholstery trim, as well as conventional silk ribbon.**

main picture: **A beaded garland can be wreathed around a present or placed on top to create a dazzling decorative detail.**

from top right: **Tiny diamanté buckles look pretty threaded onto velvet ribbon and become an additional gift—a choker or bracelet—once the present is unwrapped. Iron-on patches, such as these dainty dragonflies, have a dual purpose: they look wonderful attached to contrasting** ribbons or wrapping paper and can also be used later. These cut-glass grapes would look lovely tied around the neck of a bottle of wine, while tiny posies of paper flowers, available from sewing notions departments or crafts stores, make lovely finishing touches to wedding presents.

materials

Ensure that your gift wrapping is a cut above the rest by amassing a collection of pretty papers, ribbons, and accessories. Whenever the need to wrap something arises, you'll have an inspiring hoard from which to choose.

Get into the habit of buying attractive or unusual ribbons and papers when you see them, rather than when you need them. This makes life much easier: no more dashing to the stores at the last minute in search of something special and returning with a dull compromise. Instead, with a well-stocked box of tricks, you can focus on the fun part—deciding on what look to create.

Keep any pretty wrapping paper that you receive, even if (once you've removed torn edges) it's not that big—small sections of paper are useful for making tags, jazzing up envelopes, or wrapping small presents. The same goes for short sections of ribbon. Your wrapping kit should also include a sharp pair of scissors, and lots of

left and below right: **Build up a stock of tissue paper in lots of colors so that you have something suitable for any occasion. At the same time, keep your eyes open for sheets of really sumptuous gift wrap, such as these oriental handmade papers and metallic designs.**

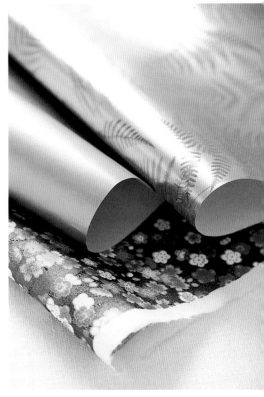

left: **Don't limit your hoarding to paper and ribbon. Fabric off-cuts are great for wrapping presents and can be made into gift bags. Small circles of fabric cut with pinking shears are perfect for covering the lids of jars, too.**

double-sided tape as well as regular Scotch tape. Keep a stock of luggage labels on hand, as they make excellent gift tags, and plain brown paper is a useful standby when inspiration fails you—it has an old-world charm that suits any situation.

Wrapping is all about concealment, and to this end you can employ scraps of fabric and wallpaper, boxes of all shapes and sizes, and smart paper bags as well as regular wrapping paper. Start a ribbon box and stock it with ribbons and fabric trims in a variety of colors and textures. Don't forget thick, rustic-looking twine and colorful raffia, or even a humble ball of string. Hold onto old buttons, buckles, and costume jewelry you've grown tired of, and press these trinkets into service as luxurious and unexpected finishing touches.

this page: **Cellophane is one of the most useful wrapping materials. It looks wonderful layered over tissue paper and gives any item a polished, professional finish.**

wrapping solutions

Not all the presents we give celebrate the big events in life. Sometimes gifts are intended as a thank you, or just to cheer someone up. This type of gift may not require elaborate wrapping, but handing over a present with little or no regard for its appearance devalues the gesture and the thought behind it. Some presents are too awkwardly shaped to wrap in a conventional manner, while others may be so elegantly packaged already that another layer of paper would be superfluous. All these situations require a slightly different wrapping solution.

tags and vouchers

A home-made tag is an easy way to add a personal touch to a small token of appreciation, and will lift the customary "thank you" box of chocolates or bottle of wine to a different level.

Parcel tags are cheap, easily available, and attractive and, with a little customizing, can be transformed into imaginative gift tags. A length of ribbon or an image cut from some wrapping paper and used to embellish a tag creates an effect that is really personal. Tags need not only adorn packages—loop them around the neck of a bottle of wine or a bunch of flowers.

Vouchers are usually well-received gifts, but a flat white envelope looks decidedly uninspiring. One solution is to buy a small gift from the same shop, which you can wrap attractively, and then attach the token to the present. Alternatively, you could insert the voucher in a handmade card and envelope crafted from luxurious decorative paper.

Vouchers are usually well-received gifts, but a flat
white envelope looks decidedly uninspiring.

food and drink

These days the packaging on edible delicacies is so stylish that, more often than not, they require no extra wrapping at all—only the addition of a pretty tag or a well-chosen accessory.

Competing with the gorgeous packaging on store-bought treats is pointless. How can you top the ornate boxes in which festive panettone is packed? Why conceal the elegant packaging on a really expensive box of handmade chocolates? Instead, use luxurious packaging as a starting point and simply fashion a personal gift tag to match, or add a charming accessory.

A jar of good olives can be teamed with a simple earthenware dish, in which they can later be served, the two tied together with rustic-looking twine or encased in a sheet of cellophane.

opposite left: **Homemade pesto looks wonderful in a chunky jar and needs only a simple label and a pretty gingham bow to make the transfer from your kitchen to someone else's pantry.**

opposite right: **A bottle of lemonade soda was chosen for its old-fashioned good looks, then dressed up with a couple of drinking glasses wrapped in cellophane, and attached with a summery ribbon.**

right: **A bottle of flavored oil is beautiful in its own right. With a hand-written label and fabric cap tied on with raffia, it needs no further embellishment.**

Don't be afraid to treat your home-made food presents in the same way as their store-bought cousins—after all, a chunky old-fashioned glass canning jar is just as stylish as any smart deli packaging. Friends will be so touched that you've taken the time to make them a jar of jam or flavored olive oil that concealing it in wrapping paper is unnecessary.

If you enjoy making preserves and cordials, get into the habit of hunting for attractive bottles and jars and look out for pretty fabrics that can be used to disguise metal lids. When it comes to labeling your gourmet creations, take care with your handwriting and think about how you can personalize the gift. You could add a tag that bears a message to the recipient of the gift, or lists the ingredients—especially helpful in this age of food allergies.

If you enjoy making preserves and cordials, get into the habit of hunting for attractive bottles and jars.

opposite: **Jellybean-filled buckets make perfect party favors, and the little bows provide a finishing touch.**

above: **A bowl filled with fortune cookies is a fun dinner-party gift, and the toy fan makes a witty tag.**

right: **A special bottle of wine is wrapped to surprise a wine buff, but funky paper and a bobble trim replaces the predictable gathered top.**

flowers and plants

Flowers and plants, bought and given for their good looks, don't need concealing. Instead, the wrapping should provide protection and act as an elegant foil for their delicate beauty.

Although many florists still use cheap paper to wrap their flowers, it doesn't take much to make even the most ordinary blooms look sensational. Once you get them home, replace the florist's wrapping with generous amounts of tissue paper and shiny cellophane, and secure with raffia or ribbon. Choose colors that complement the flowers, and make sure that the bow is big and bold. Vibrant hot-pink tissue paper looks funky wrapped around acid-green chrysanthemums, while paler shades emphasize the delicate nature of orchids and their satiny petals, and ordinary brown wrapping paper is neutral enough to suit most flowers, from the sculptural simplicity of a few bold stems to the most lavish bouquet.

left and above: **A small bunch of orchids becomes an extravagant-looking gesture when tied with sumptuous ribbons chosen to complement the throat of the flowers. A bloom that was slightly damaged during wrapping is used as an elegant finishing touch (above).**

left: **Simple brown paper has been done a million times over, and with good reason—it works.**
above: **Treat potted plants in the same way as bouquets. Bunch colored tissue paper around them, then tie with raffia.**

It doesn't take much to make even the most ordinary blooms look sensational.

special occasions

Special occasions such as weddings and birthdays offer great opportunities for really creative wrapping. Although no one feels disappointed when presented with a gift, it's undeniably more exciting to be handed a package all dressed up to reflect a specific occasion. The approach you take is up to you, but bear in mind the recipient's tastes, too—would they prefer a present that's wittily wrapped or a more sophisticated style? And don't let a present's size restrict your creativity: a tiny package crowned with a vast ribbon can be just as enticing as a huge box.

left: **Conjure up the effect of a festive snowfall by using fluffy snowflake tree decorations in place of gift tags. Unusual trimmings, such as this string of white sequins, make a great alternative to the conventional satin ribbon.**

below and opposite, above right: **Rather than wrapping every present in the same paper, choose a variety of papers with similar patterns and colors, then use a scattering of tree decorations to unify the theme.**

christmas

No one can fail to be excited by a stack of presents piled high at the bottom of the Christmas tree. The fun of unwrapping them is as important as the gifts themselves, so take the time to make your presents look good.

Every year we bemoan the increasing commercialization of Christmas, so perhaps extolling the virtues of lavish gift wrapping may go against the grain. But taking care over the way in which you wrap your presents, and investing time and thought in making them look good, will mean that the lucky recipients will not only be more careful as they unwrap their gifts, but they will also have a greater appreciation for the contents.

Certainly for children, unwrapping Christmas presents is so much fun that, more often than not, the actual gift is given no more than a cursory glance before being tossed to one side in order to grapple with the next one. But pretty wrapping paper, elaborate bows, and amusing trinkets used in place of cards and tags will ensure that

right: **A homemade paper bag is given a stylish seal with a crystal chandelier drop tied to a ribbon. For details of how to make similar bags, see page 58.**

below, left and right: **This bold Deco-inspired paper has been dressed up with deliciously tactile pinky-gray velvet ribbons and diamanté buckles to create a glamorous effect.**

above and right: **It's not just the rich colors of these wrapping papers that gives these presents their seductive look. It's also the range of textures: paper, silk, and glass.**

Imaginative gift tags are another guaranteed way to make your presents stand out from the crowd.

far right: **A piece of sumptuous silk has been used to wrap a very special gift. Traditional Chinese silk buttons have been glued on as a finishing touch, though the fabric is really secured with double-sided tape.**

main picture: **A bag is dressed up with ribbons, a silk bloom, and pretty paper to hide any logos.**

family present-giving and unwrapping sessions proceed at a slower, more decorous pace!

One way to make sure your presents create an impact is to theme the way in which you wrap them. Don't restrict yourself to just one style of paper—wrap presents in perhaps four different papers in complementary colors, so that when viewed en masse your gifts look almost too good to open. A pile of presents wrapped in shades of white and cream, sparkling with highlights of silver and gold and tied with different-textured ribbons, will create the impression of a magical snowdrift underneath the tree.

Imaginative gift tags are another way to make your presents stand out from the crowd. There's a huge

One way to ensure your presents create an impact is to theme the way in which you wrap them.

variety of Christmas decorations on the market and they're becoming more affordable, too. If you change the look of your tree each year, recycle old decorations as gift tags—clusters of bright baubles look stunning looped onto ribbons and tied around packages. A step on from using decorations to adorn your presents is to attach something to the front that provides a clue to the contents. A bundle of candles tied with a bow and attached to a box containing a set of candlesticks not only looks chic but adds to the pleasure and surprise of the unwrapping.

above left: **A fat tassel that matches the background of this hand-printed paper is an excellent alternative to a bow.**

above center: **Brown paper looks chic with the addition of plaid ribbon and a posy of eucalyptus and rosemary sprigs.**

above right: **A simple box-shaped present wrapped in plain tissue paper is enlivened with a bright candy cane and jingle-bell ribbons, while the present wrapped in the jolly garland paper is finished with a witty bunch of artificial red cherries.**

opposite: **A bundle of candles atop a glossy package provides a clue as to its contents.**

above and left: **Look in crafts stores and sewing notions departments for unusual ribbons and details such as this sequined butterfly. Choose things your mother will enjoy using later.**

opposite, left and right: **A heart-shaped lavender bag not only looks lovely against the delicate *toile de Jouy* wrapping paper, but forms part of the present, too.**

mother's day

If there is one person who is guaranteed to appreciate the care you take over wrapping their present, it's your mom. Handing over an exquisitely wrapped treat says so much more about your feelings for her than the predictable card and bunch of flowers.

Coming as it does, in late spring, soft pastel colors are the obvious choices when selecting wrapping paper for Mother's Day presents. Soft blues, lavenders, yellows, and pinks always look pretty and are perfectly suited to the more traditional Mother's Day presents such as luxury soaps, scented candles, and chocolates.

But if your gift is a little more unusual, or you feel that these pale, sugared-almond colors are too obvious, look for wrapping papers with motifs your mother might appreciate. Does she love chintzy floral patterns? Or is she mad about cats? Easier still, you could choose paper in various shades of her favorite color and decorate the present with a scattering of pretty silk flowers or dainty sequined butterflies. Alternatively, you could take

inspiration from the present itself—a book about flowers or gardening would be lovely wrapped in floral paper, while a piece of jewelry could be placed in a box that you have customized in some way that hints at the contents. If the present is a gift token of some sort—for a day of pampering at a spa, say—you could attach the voucher to a bunch of flowers or slip it into a handmade envelope bag (see page 58) along with an additional treat such as a luxury lipstick.

If you can't decide upon a particular theme, then pretty tissue paper is always a safe bet. Incredibly cheap, and available in a wide range of colors, tissue paper is an excellent fallback and means that you can really go to town with the finishing touches: organza ribbons, feather butterflies, and imitation flowers.

Decorate the present with a scattering of pretty silk flowers or dainty sequined butterflies.

opposite: **Pale aqua paper is the perfect background for a striking bronze ribbon, while the delicate organza bow echoes the leaf-skeleton motif on the dark gray paper.**

left and above: **Hot pinky-red ribbon on red paper is an eyecatching and exotic combination, especially with the addition of the vibrant feather butterflies.**

left: **Two lengths of ribbon used together disguise the fact that both are too short to encircle the present completely!**

below: **A lipstick attached to the front of this present is a fun reference to the Cupid's-bow design on the paper.**

valentine's day

Valentine's Day gifts are not restricted to lavish declarations of grand passions— they also include light-hearted little treats given to those you care about most.

For die-hard romantics, Valentine's Day is the perfect excuse for some really audacious gift wrapping. Although many of the stores specializing in the luxury trinkets we tend to give on Valentine's Day offer excellent gift-wrapping services, don't deny yourself an opportunity to shine. The way you present your gift is, after all, an expression of your feelings, and what better way to get your message across than with a carefully chosen, lovingly wrapped present?

Hot reds and vibrant pinks are the colors of the day, but if these don't feel appropriate— particularly when wrapping a present for a man— consider the whole red-to-pink spectrum, which

left and above: **Drop a few homemade chocolates (or cheat with fancy store-bought truffles) into cellophane bags tied with pretty ribbons—a perfect Valentine's Day treat for best friends, favorite aunts, or even your children.**

What better way to get your message across than with a carefully chosen, lovingly wrapped present?

also includes masculine burgundies and rich eggplant-colored tones. These darker colors are not as feminine as scarlet and pink, yet have suitably passionate associations.

Stores are usually brimming with Valentine-themed gift wrap as soon as Christmas is over, and this can be fun to work with. Wrapping paper decorated with pouting lips or cutesy love hearts captures the kitsch aspect of this celebration, and can be just the thing for more light-hearted expressions of love.

Your Valentine's Day presents may be simply small tokens of affection, and this is when a hoard of pretty scraps of fabric, small pieces of wrapping paper, and odd lengths of ribbon will come into its own. Those little boxes that you've saved during the year can be personalized and filled with luxury chocolates, or you can make up lots of little cellophane bags of truffles and tie each with a pretty ribbon and a message of love.

Wrapping paper decorated with pouting lips or love hearts captures the kitsch aspect of this celebration.

opposite: **An outsize bow on a tiny box hints at the significance of the gift.**

left: **Lacy paper layered over soft white tissue suggests that lingerie lies inside, as does the frilly garter-style ribbon.**

above: **Elegant store packaging needs little else to enhance it, but a lavish decorative bow keeps the lid on until the day.**

left and below: **This might have been just another prettily wrapped box, but the sumptuous gold and white paper, wide ribbon, and the addition of the cup and saucer on top (part of the set contained inside), makes it really stand out.**

weddings

With so many couples using wedding lists, few receive anything other than boxes stamped with a department store logo. Be different—go to town on your wrapping and give your friends a treat.

Weddings can be wildly romantic or simply wild parties, but whatever they are, they're rarely dull, and the way you wrap your presents should reflect the magic of the occasion. By using gold, silver, and white wrapping, you will be alluding to the central elements of the big day—the ring, the dress, and the romance of the occasion. Add interest in the form of ribbons and silk flowers, or, if it's a set of some sort, even use part of the present as a decorative detail tied to the top.

The bride and groom are not the only people to receive presents at a wedding. Traditionally, members of the wedding party, such as

left and above: **Traditional gold and white wedding gift wrap is given a more personal touch with the addition of beautiful ribbons. Party favors for the guests have been tied with ribbons that echo the colors of the day—the bride's bouquet and the bridesmaids' dresses.**

By using gold, silver, and white wrapping, you will be alluding to the central elements of the big day.

above: **These delicate fabric roses are discreetly pinned to a length of finely graded ribbon to create an exquisite finishing touch.**

above right: **A miniature bouquet of dainty paper flowers is a charming detail well suited to a wedding present or a gift for a bridesmaid.**

opposite left: **The gift wrap and ribbon on this box containing a set of antique cutlery echo the pattern on the handles of the forks.**

opposite right: **A thank-you present for the maid of honor is wrapped in paper that tones with her dress, and is finished with roses used in her bouquet.**

bridesmaids, groomsmen, and flower girls, are given small gifts to thank them for their participation. The mothers of the bride and groom are often given flowers, and it's increasingly common for couples to give party favors, which are also used for decorating each place setting. It's worth taking the time to make these tokens of appreciation look good. The obvious approach is to select wrapping paper and ribbons that reflect the colors of the bride's bouquet and the bridesmaids' dresses. Little white tissue-paper packages tied with prettily colored ribbons look charming and take next to no time to prepare. Little boxes of sugared almonds or jellybeans in pastel shades are inexpensive and easy to organize, yet look fantastically chic.

The obvious approach is to select paper and ribbons that reflect the colors of the bride's bouquet.

opposite: **Gadgets always go down well, and here a keyring fastening is used to secure the two ends of silver twine.**

far left: **This clever intertwining of luscious velvet ribbon (see page 60) avoids the need for a feminine-looking bow, while still providing a necessary flourish.**

left: **A simple envelope-style package is made more interesting with the addition of a tag decorated to match the paper.**

gifts for men

Although they may not want their presents dressed up with bows and silk flowers, the men in your life are sure to appreciate a present that's stylishly wrapped. Aim for a look that is both witty and bold, and remember that little gadgets always go down well.

Most men hate the business of wrapping up presents, and this can make wrapping a gift for your partner feel like a waste of time. But hand a man a gift wrapped in witty paper that alludes to his hobby, or one topped off with an amusing gadget, and he'll see the light. And if this extra effort means that you get a lovely-looking present in return, then it's an effort worth making.

As a starting point, consider what the present is celebrating—a birthday, Christmas, or a new job? Take inspiration from the occasion and use this as the basis for your wrapping scheme. For someone off on a city break or a trip around the world, a map of his destination will make excellent wrapping paper. Older men, such as fathers and grandfathers, may appreciate a

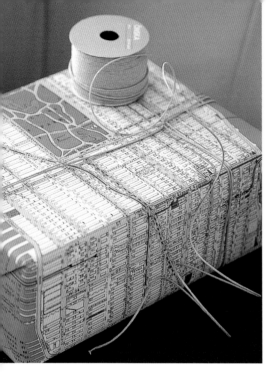

left: **A map of downtown Manhattan neatly tied with thin parcel string is a fantastic way to wrap a couple of travel books for an inveterate globetrotter.**

below: **A luggage tag embellished with a subway ticket complements this London Tube-map paper. The red and yellow ties were cut from clothesline.**

more old-fashioned approach, such as heavy parchment paper sealed with thick grosgrain ribbon and sealing wax. Wrapping paper that reflects the recipient's interests is always a winner, raising a smile even before they've opened the present. Bold, abstract designs or funky, colorful psychedelic swirls are undeniably stylish. And, although silky ribbon may seem a vital part of any wrapping, a big bow on a gift for a man can seem a little off key. Twine, leather ties, or looping a keyring fastening through a piece of ribbon, however, are suitably masculine alternatives.

Traditional approaches always go down well. The hand-marbled envelope bag (see page 58) with its matching tassel looks chic and classic, as does the gift wrapped in soft parchment paper and finished with old-fashioned sealing wax and tape.

Textured snakeskin-patterned paper secured with strands of suede from an old belt is perfect for a man given to Crocodile Dundee-style adventures.

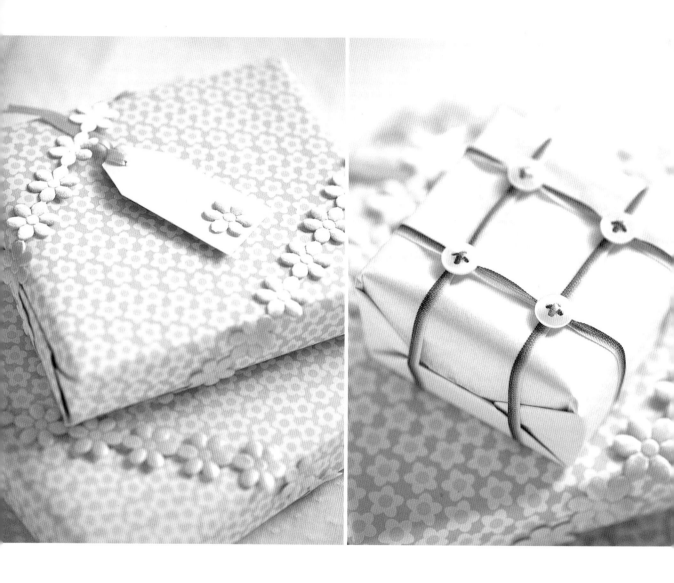

Give in to temptation and team the prettiest papers
you can find with delicate ribbons and dainty trims.

opposite left: **A piece of the dainty daisy trim from the package is used to adorn a matching gift tag.** opposite right and below left: **This is a lovely way to wrap a present for** someone who enjoys sewing, as the buttons can be used later. Four pieces of fine ribbon are threaded through mother-of-pearl buttons and secured at the back of the package. below: **Some first books for baby are wrapped in delicate marbled paper in the traditional colors of babyhood (for instructions on wrapping books, see page 59).**

new baby

Presents for newborns are more truthfully treats for their mothers, who will get far more pleasure from tiny cashmere cardigans and bobble hats than the baby ever will. The same is true of dainty, delicate gift wrapping, which new moms will really appreciate, too.

Why fight the traditional pastel colors associated with newborns when they are so well suited to the delicate and pretty presents we tend to give: tiny hats and first teddy bears? Instead, give in to temptation and team the prettiest papers you can find with delicate ribbons and dainty trims. Soft toys don't even need wrapping; a Paddington Bear-style luggage label tied on with a big blue or pink bow will suffice.

Although it's traditional to make a present for a friend's new baby, the reality is that nowadays few of us have time for knitting and sewing, and fewer still actually know how to. Instead, you can do the next best thing—go to town with the wrapping paper and have fun making pretty tags to match.

left: **This package wrapped in comic cow paper is decorated with a matching keyring—a detail that's guaranteed to slow the pace of the unwrapping. The pink ribbon was chosen to match the cows' noses.**

below: **A rubber frog with an extendable tongue is a fun gift topper. The package has been secured with a length of name tape, which has been printed with the age of the recipient.**

gifts for children

It may seem pointless to make much effort with a child's present when it will be unwrapped again in the blink of an eye, but a present topped with an appealing trinket or wrapped in eyecatching paper will be handled with a little more respect!

When wrapping gifts for kids, selecting a theme is easy. Either go for paper that relates to the contents of the package (pink and girly if it's a Barbie, or something rugged in khaki if it's a G.I. Joe) or the theme of the party. All children enjoy jokes and tricks, so placing the present inside a container that suggests it might be something else is an easy way to add an unexpected bit of excitement to the proceedings—try rolling the item up in a page of the Sunday comics. Children also love fiddly little bits and pieces, so decorating a gift with a novelty trinket such as a keyring, a small bag of chocolate buttons, or a lollipop is always a huge success.

right: **Going-home bags, as every parent knows, are an absolutely unavoidable part of any birthday party. Here, orange and black Hallowe'en bags are finished off with home-made tags (wrapping paper stuck to card stock), which are attached to the bags with orange pipe-cleaners.**

below: **This bold and sophisticated Chinese paper is given a more child-friendly finish with a traditional paper dragon puppet attached across the middle of the gift.**

below: **The large chocolate bunnies available at Eastertime present a real surprise for small children when boxed and then wrapped in bright tissue paper and tied with fat gingham bows. A lollipop stuck into the bow is a sticky bonus!**

As all parents know, going-home bags are an essential ingredient of a successful birthday party. They actually become much more fun to put together if you embrace the inevitable and get creative with their contents and appearance. There are lots of excellent children's catalogs around these days. All of them have party sections from which you can buy tiny toys and other silly tricks and novelties, along with plain but colorful bags to customize in line with your child's chosen party theme, whether it be pirates, princesses, or fairies.

left and above: **What better way to deal with G.I. Joe than wrapping him in commando-style camouflage paper? Boys quickly turn against bows, so bright-orange raffia has been used instead.**

Going-home bags are more fun to put together if you get creative with their contents and appearance.

wrapping boxes

Boxes are probably the easiest things to wrap, so if you're giving an awkwardly shaped gift, putting it in a box first is a good solution. The hard edges allow you to create professional-looking, neat packages.

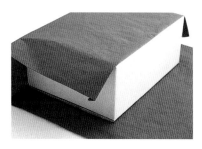

1 Place the box face down in the center of the wrapping paper, pull up the long sides (above), and secure, one on top of the other, with a short piece of Scotch tape.

2 Turn the present the right way up and carefully fold down the overhanging paper against the two sides of the box that remain exposed (right).

3 Press in two side folds, smoothing the edges to give a clean finish. Next, fold over the very end of the bottom flap (above), then fold it up to cover all the edges and create an envelope effect. Secure with tape or a decorative sticker. Turn over and repeat the process at the other end.

wrapping bottles

Wrapping bottles is not difficult, but it is worth taking a little time to achieve a neat, crisp finish.

1 Roll your bottle in wrapping paper as if you were wrapping a cylinder (see opposite page). Neatly pleat the paper at the base and secure with tape (left).

2 Carefully fold in the excess paper at the neck of the bottle to create a point or a blunt edge that can be folded over like the flap of an envelope and secured with tape.

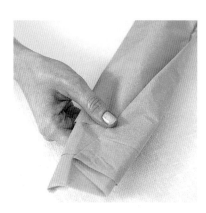

wrapping cylinders

This wrapping method suits cylindrical objects such as jars and bottles. It can also be used for disguising a present's shape—roll the item up in a cardboard tube, then wrap it. Tissue or crêpe paper works best for this style of wrapping, as it is easy to fold neatly.

1 Cut a piece of paper longer than the cylinder at each end. Roll the paper tightly around the gift and secure with tape, leaving the ends free.

2 Start to pleat the paper neatly towards the center of the gift (above), making precise, narrow, overlapping folds.

3 Pleat all the way around the diameter of the gift, releasing the first folds as necessary to allow you to continue the pleats all the way around (above).

4 Gently interleaf the folds to create a perfect concertina effect. Secure with tape or a decorative sticker (above). Turn over and repeat the process at the other end.

envelope bags

Gift bags can be used for all types of things, from a pair of cashmere socks to a silk scarf or a luxurious designer lipstick. Stiff paper or thin card stock is best for an envelope bag, as it provides more structure and support.

1 Fold over your paper so it overlaps, then secure with tape. Make a deep fold at one end (above). This will form the bottom of the bag.

2 Gently pull open your fold and flatten it out, creasing the paper so a sharp point is formed at each end (above).

3 Bend in the edges of the fold so they meet in the middle (above), then secure with a small piece of tape.

4 Fold in the sides so the pointed ends dovetail with the edges of the fold (right). Secure with tape.

5 Carefully open out the bottom of the bag and gently form creases along each side (right).

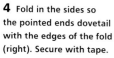

handmade envelopes

handmade envelopes are an elegant way to wrap tickets, vouchers, gloves, ties, or even jewelry, which can first be wrapped in tissue paper. Choose heavyweight paper, or back your chosen paper with thin card stock.

Take a standard envelope in whichever size you need and very carefully undo it, lay it flat on your chosen paper, and use it as a template. Draw around the outline, cut it out, and glue together (left). If your present is too big or small for a standard envelope, you can make your own by scaling a standard envelope up or down and marking the measurements onto the back of your chosen paper. As a finishing touch, stickers or other lightweight fastenings can be glued into place (right).

wrapping books

Books can very easily be wrapped in the same way as boxes (see page 56), but a more interesting method is to fold the edges of the wrapping paper into the books themselves. Soft handmade papers are particularly good for this, and double-sided tape is essential for a sleek finish.

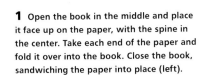

1 Open the book in the middle and place it face up on the paper, with the spine in the center. Take each end of the paper and fold it over into the book. Close the book, sandwiching the paper into place (left).

2 Fold the corners of the loose ends inwards as you would when wrapping a box using the conventional method. Turn the flap up onto the underside of the present and secure with tape (right).

securing ribbons

Although you would think that tying a length of ribbon around a present is hardly rocket science, it can be surprisingly tricky, and a practice run before you cut into your ribbon will save on waste. Everyone knows how to tie bows—the classic finishing touch—but this arrangement of thick ribbon looped together and doubled back on itself is a smart alternative and just as easy to create. To get the best results, use double-sided sticky tape, as sheer or silky ribbon invariably slips.

1 Sit your package on top of your length of ribbon. Take the two ends of the ribbon and hook them around each other to form two interlocking loops. Pull the ends back underneath the gift.

2 Carefully turn the present over and secure the two ends of the ribbon flat against the bottom of the package with Scotch tape and, if you want, a decorative sticker.

3 Turn the present the right side up and very gently fan the ribbon out so that all four strips are visible, as in the picture (right). Tiny strips of double-sided tape stuck under the ribbon at either end will keep it in place and stop it from slipping.

finishing touches

Once the wrapping paper is in place, it's time to have fun with the final flourishes, such as ribbons and pretty trinkets. When choosing what to use, consider color, scale, and the sort of thing the recipient would like best.

right: **For a ruffle bow, take a length of ribbon and fold it backwards and forwards to create a concertina effect, but decreasing the size of the ruffle each time. Finish off with a full loop in the center. Fasten with a pin or stick each layer down with double-sided tape. Attach to the gift with double-sided tape.**

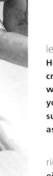

above: **Attaching a paper posy or lollipop to a present with a bow is a lovely finishing touch and incredibly easy. Tie your ribbon around the present and knot it, then place the posy or lollipop across the knot and tie your bow.**

left: **When tying a bow, consider scale. Here, a silk bow dominates the box and creates a luscious, lavish feel. Thin ribbon would look meager in comparison. Once you've tied your bow, tweak it, making sure it is correctly positioned and as full as possible before you trim the ends.**

right: **Trimming the ends of your ribbons, either to an asymmetric point or into a fork, may seem unnecessary, but attention to detail gives a professional finish.**

sources

A.I. Friedman
431 Boston Port Road
Port Chester, NY 10573
800-204-6352
www.aifriedman.com
*Also shop their online store for beautiful
specialty paper products.*

Alphabétique
701 W. Armitage Avenue
Chicago, IL 60614
312-751-2920
www.alphabetiquechicago.com
*Specialty wrap, ribbons, vintage gift-toppers,
tags, and more.*

The Art Store
Locations nationwide.
Visit www.artstore.com for details of your
nearest store.
A huge selection of quality art supplies.

Carlton Cards
Locations nationwide.
Visit www.carltoncards.com for details of
your nearest store.
Cards and gift wrap for every holiday.

The Container Store
Locations nationwide.
Visit www.containerstore.com for details of
your nearest store.
Gift boxes, bags, paper, ribbon, and more.

Cost Plus World Market
Locations nationwide.
Visit www.costplus.com for details of your
nearest store.
*A specialty retailer that carries decorative
papers from around the world.*

Dick Blick Art Materials
Locations throughout the Midwest.
Visit www.dickblick.com for details of your
nearest store.
*A huge variety of crepe, tissue, and decorative
paper; stencils, ribbon, and more.*

Expressions With Heart
107 High Ave. West
Oskaloosa, IA 52577
866-672-1730
www.expressionswithheart.com
Paper, stamps, stencils, and beads, ribbons.

Flax Art & Design
1699 Market Street
San Francisco, CA 94103
415-552-2355
www.flaxart.com
Creative paper, ribbons, and art supplies.

Hallmark
Locations nationwide.
Visit www.hallmark.com for details of your
nearest store.
Greeting cards, gift wrap, and more.

Heirloom Woven Labels
Box 428-IN
Moorestown, NJ 08057
856-722-1618
www.heirloomlabels.com
High-quality, durable woven labels.

Jam Paper
111 Third Avenue
New York, NY 10003
Call 212-473-6666 or visit www.jampaper.com
for details of their other stores.
*Extensive mail-order and online catalogue
service, supply specialty paper, ribbons,
envelopes, and packaging.*

JoAnn Fabrics
Locations nationwide.
Visit www.joann.com for details of your
nearest store.
A superstore for fabric and craft materials.

Kate's Paperie
561 Broadway
New York, NY 10012
212-941-9816
Visit www.katespaperie.com for details of
your nearest store.
*Five stores in New York and Connecticut
feature specialty papers and stationery.*

McLaughlin Paper Company
Design Studio & Showroom:
80 Progress Avenue
West Springfield, MA 01089
800-842-6656
www.mclaughlinpaper.com
*Quality specialty printed papers, foil,
decorative tissue, and holographic designs.*

New York Central Art Supply
62 Third Avenue
New York, NY 10003
800-950-6111
www.nycentralart.com
A huge selection of excellent-quality papers.

Only the Best
15954 Los Gatos Blvd
Los Gatos, CA 95032
408-356-7362
www.onlythebestlosgatos.com
Specialty paper products, stamps, and stencils.

picture credits

Paper Access
23 West 18th Street
New York, NY 10011
800-PAPER-01
www.paperaccess.com
*Handmade and specialty paper, wraps,
ribbon, gift tags, cards, and accessories.*

Papyrus
Locations nationwide.
Visit www.papyrusonline.com for details of
your nearest store.
Cards, paper, ribbon, and gift wrap.

Party and Paper Warehouse, Inc.
5107 Rowlett Road
Rowlett, TX 75088
972-463-1991
www.partyandpaperwarehouse.com
A huge selection of party supplies and papers.

Party City
Locations nationwide.
Visit www.partycity.com for details of your
nearest store.
A reliable source for wrapping supplies.

Potpourri Paper
206-972-2326
www.potpourrionline.com
*An online distributor of handmade papers,
stationery, journals, art and gift supplies.*

The Sweet Palace
109 East Broadway
Philipsburg, MT 59858
888-793-3896
www.sweetpalace.com
*A huge selection of old-fashioned candies and
suckers available to buy online. Their suckers
and swizzles will appeal to any kid!*

Target
Locations nationwide.
Visit www.target.com for details of your
nearest store.
Gift wrap, ornaments, and decorations.

Thompson Paper
215 Southwest Boulevard
Kansas City, MO 64108
877-827-2737
www.handmadepapers.emerchantpro.com
Handmade papers, vellum, ribbon, and more.

Twinrocker Handmade Paper
100 East Third Street
P.O. Box 413
Brookston, IN 47923
800-757-8946
www.twinrocker.com
*Handmade papers from the finest cotton and
linen rag.*

Utrecht
Stores nationwide.
Visit www.utrechtart.com for details of your
nearest store.
Discount art supplies.

Walgreens
Locations nationwide.
Visit www.walgreens.com for details of your
nearest store.
Good for last-minute wrapping supplies.

30 Zago Papers
137 East Palace
Santa Fe, NM 87501-2010
505-988-9246
www.zagopapers.com
*Handmade papers from around the world,
including Japanese mulberry, Egyptian
papyrus, and Thai tamarind leaves.*

acknowledgments

I would especially like to thank Carolyn Barber for her
exquisite photography—she not only produced beautiful
pictures, but was also an absolute pleasure to work
with. I would also like to thank my family, David, Sadie,
Hannah, and Lottie, for their continuing support and
inspiration. Thank you to Annabelle Lewis of
VV Rouleaux, for her extreme generosity—without her
fabulous ribbons, the packages would simply not come
alive. Thanks also to Amanda at Flirty, for her beautiful
flowers. Thank you to Jacob, and his little friends, Lily
and Violet, who look so adorable in the book, and
lastly to Gabriella, Sally, and everyone at RPS.